A Tas...
Chicken Soup for the Soul

Teacher Tales
Inspirational Stories from
Great Teachers and Appreciative Students

Jack Canfield
Mark Victor Hansen
Amy Newmark

CSS

Chicken Soup for the Soul Publishing, LLC

Cos Cob, CT

A Taste of Chicken Soup for the Soul Teacher Tales
Inspirational Stories from Great Teachers and Appreciative Students
By Jack Canfield, Mark Victor Hansen & Amy Newmark

Published by Chicken Soup for the Soul Publishing, LLC
www.chickensoup.com

Cover illustration courtesy of iStockPhoto.com/procurator/
© Evgeniy Ivanov. Cover photo courtesy of
iStockPhoto.com/luminis.

Library of Congress Control Number: 2013940464

A Taste of ISBN: 978-1-61159-857-5
Full Book ISBN: 978-1-935096-47-4

Contents

Bring Me Back a Rock

Man is harder than rock and more fragile
than an egg.
~Yugoslav Proverb

Seven years have gone by now, yet in my mind's eye I can still vividly recall every detail as if it happened yesterday. Your small round face, never quite clean enough, stringy blond bangs hanging over sad brown eyes. Clothes always wrinkled and too small on your bony shoulders, and sockless feet inside worn-out sneakers with no shoelaces. You maintained an almost invisible identity, always fearful of others who whispered as you walked by and nicknamed you "rag muffin."

Having a daughter your exact age made my heart ache for you even more. What if I couldn't afford the things for my little girl that your parents couldn't provide for you and your five brothers and sisters? I wanted to do something to help but I didn't know how or what I could do. Besides, I was just your teacher. And then from out of nowhere it hit me—that's what I can do. Along with teaching you reading and math and spelling, I'll teach you some everyday skills that might improve the quality of your life and other people's perception of you.

First I had to reverse your self-induced disappearing act and make you visible again. Others needed to see the real you, a seven-year-old boy who didn't always behave himself but who always said he was sorry when he didn't. I brought to school a grooming bag complete with soap, towel, comb, toothbrush and toothpaste and discretely sent you to the boys' room every morning to get cleaned up. I appealed to my friends who had little boys to give me their hand-me-down clothes and shoes. Sneaking crackers into your backpack for snack time and secretly paying for you to have "doubles" in the school cafeteria became everyday rituals.

Our classroom became your home away from home, your safe haven, a place where you could escape and be a child, at least for a little while. Then at 3:00 PM the dismissal bell would ring. And like the midnight gong that interrupted Cinderella's dance at the ball, I gave you a goodbye hug and smile and sent you back to your world. The world where, hopefully unlike what happened to Cinderella, I prayed you wouldn't change back into a ragamuffin.

I worried about you all the time, even on the weekends. I remember one cool, crisp North Carolina Saturday morning, right before the weather turned cold; my daughter and I went out shopping for her new winter coat. This was an annual battle we had engaged in since she was four years old. For me the perfect winter coat had to be long and wool and thick enough to shield her from the winds that got bitter cold from the months of December to March. An attached hood would also be nice, since leaving home wearing a cap didn't necessarily mean she'd come home with it.

In her eyes, the perfect winter coat had only requirement. It had to be pink. After many hours and hundreds of try-ons we finally found a coat we could both agree on. It was long, thick, hooded, and yes, it was pink.

Filled with a sense of accomplishment, all I wanted to do was pay for the coat and hurry home to curl up on the couch with a good girly movie or book. Instead, for reasons beyond my understanding, I grabbed the pink coat in one hand and my daughter's hand in the other and said, "Now we have to go to the boys department and buy a coat for Johnnie."

That's what life was like for us during the two years I was your teacher. But it was worth it. Things were definitely looking up for you. You gained weight, you smiled more and you even began to risk raising your hand in class to answer questions. You trusted me enough to know I would always lead you to the correct answer. But your trust in others was still a little shaky and it was time to fix that, especially since you would be promoted to the next grade and you weren't going to be my student next year.

I began to plan partner projects and group activities that required you to communicate with your classmates and work as a team. At first, you refused to work with anyone else but me and you even got mad at me when I insisted you work with someone else. But with a lot of time and a lot of coaxing you eventually started to relax and have trust in your peers.

That is until one cool breezy fall day in November, the last school day before the Thanksgiving holiday. The classroom buzzed with the electricity of children hardly able to contain their excitement. All they could think about were the intriguing adventures awaiting them over the holiday. By afternoon, with only one more hour of school, no one was in the mood for learning. So I ditched the video of *The First Thanksgiving*, which they had seen every November since kindergarten, and instead decided to have a sharing time where everyone got a chance to tell about their plans for the upcoming holiday.

You sat in your usual place, right next to me, and listened while your peers told about cruises to the Bahamas, trips to Disneyland and visits to Grandma in New York and other faraway places. With no one else left to share, I turned to you and asked, "Johnnie, would you like to tell us what you're doing over the Thanksgiving holiday?"

"Yes," you said proudly. "I'm going to Kernersville to visit my aunt." The words were barely out of your mouth when the class erupted with laughter. Everyone knew Kernersville, about twenty minutes outside of Winston-Salem, was nowhere special to go. You froze in embarrassment and began to retreat back inside yourself.

I rushed to your rescue, "REALLY!" I yelled out over the laughter. "Would you bring me back a-a-a rock," I stuttered. "I could really use a nice rock." The room became perfectly still with an uncomfortable silence as you silently nodded, "Yes, Mrs. Reynolds."

Thanksgiving break, like all vacations, ended much too soon. Children returned to school with stories, pictures and items to share, each child trying to outdo the other with tall tales and embellished stories. This time I knew better than to put the spotlight on you and ask you to share, but without warning you stood up and began to slowly walk to the front of the room. The shock and fear I felt for you made me hold my breath so hard, I believe my heart actually skipped a beat. For a moment you just stood there looking down at your feet and then without saying a word, you reached into your coat pocket and pulled out a rock. A rock washed and polished until it shined like a new penny, a rock just small enough for two tiny trembling hands to hold. A rock that neither you nor I could possibly know would change our hearts forever.

The entire class silently awaited my reaction. They were obviously confused and taking their cues from me on how to react. "WOW!" I said, reaching out with the kind of hands used to hold a newborn infant or something priceless and delicate. "It's absolutely perfect. This is exactly the kind of rock I was hoping for. Please tell us all about it."

Hesitantly, you began to tell about the rock—where you found it—why you chose it. With every word, your voice grew stronger and your stance grew taller. At long last, all eyes and ears belonged to you. At the conclusion of your share, classmates applauded with enthusiasm and someone yelled out, "Johnnie, YOU ROCK." I watched you like a proud mother bird watches her baby bird take flight for the very first time. I knew it was time to let you go.

Finally, you had found your wings and it was time for you to soar.

Needless to say I received many rocks that year. So many that we began a classroom rock collection. Some rocks came from volcanic mountains and underground canyons. Other rocks came from local restaurants or a relative's backyard. Every rock had a story and earned another pushpin on the map. By the end of the school year the class had collected nearly fifty rocks and had learned more about the world and themselves than any number of books could have ever taught them. Students from other classrooms came to know us as the rock experts and you, Johnnie, you were the rock master.

As fate would have it, your family moved away that summer and left no forwarding address. So I never got to see you again or say goodbye. But the rock tradition continues. Every year I tell the story of "bring me back a rock" to my new class of students. I tell them that all rocks from previous class collections are boxed up and put away except for the rock inside this clear plastic cube. This rock has a permanent place on my desk and in my heart. As I hold up the rock I explain that it may look ordinary and insignificant but it's by far the most precious rock of them all. This rock represents love, courage and acceptance of others. It is the very rock that started it all and it was given to me by someone who will always be near and dear to my heart.

Thanks Johnnie, and wherever you are, "bring me back a rock."

~Adrienne C. Reynolds

The Glitter Mask

Every artist dips his brush in his own soul,
and paints his own nature into his pictures.
~Henry Ward Beecher

It is Tuesday, just three days before Halloween. We have been making Halloween masks in my first class of the day, and I need to quickly clear and organize feathers, sequins and glue bottles before rushing on to my next class.

Quiany sidles up to me. In the wheedling tone she uses when attempting to manipulate you into doing something "just for her" she asks, "Can I use some more glitter, Miss Miller? Can I use more sequins? Just a little more. I know you always say that with glitter, less is more. But just a little more, Miss Miller? Please?"

I say, "We'll see, Quiany. But not today. I'll be back with your class again on Thursday afternoon. We'll just have to see."

"Okay, Miss Miller. Okay."

Though I have a lot of life experience, with a family and fully developed corporate career in my past, I am a brand new teacher in a tough New York City school district and still feeling things out. I'm not sure of the right way to handle so many situations, and this is one of those.

As things turn out, I am not at work on Thursday afternoon, when I would ordinarily be teaching Quiany's class again. My first grandchild, a girl, is born Wednesday night and I spend Thursday in the hospital with Alexis and beautiful new Ruby Jane. On Friday, when I return to school, it's Halloween and our little school of students with special needs is even wilder than usual. Students are excited, and way out of control.

Since I keep some of my art materials in a cabinet in my friend Mari's room, I go there first to get myself set up for my classes. Quiany, as it happens, has been placed in Mari's classroom for the day, probably to keep her out of harm's way. Streetwise and manipulative though Quiany may be, the pre-adolescent boys in her class of complicated nine- to eleven-year-olds are leagues beyond her in that department. On the other hand, the five- and six-year-old developmentally delayed students in Mari's class, though challenging for the teachers, can be very sweet and they love Quiany a lot, and she loves them. Today, this is definitely a better place for her to be.

As soon as she sees me, Quiany comes over from the dress-up corner, where she has been playing with Starr. She is wearing a tall, pointed witch's hat covered in black sequins. In her slightly accented voice, so softly I can barely hear her, she asks, "Miss Miller, can I work on my mask? Can I use a little glitter?"

"That's okay with me today, Quiany, but

let's make sure it's okay with Miss Mari."

It was.

"Okay, Quiany, I'll get your mask and some materials, and you'll be able to use a little glitter."

In a few minutes, I return with Quiany's mask and some materials she can add to her mask. I also have my toolbox, which contains, among other things, the glitter she is so focused on. But before I can get everything arranged, I hear screaming from another classroom. It is my job to check out situations like this, so I need to go see what I can do to help. I tell Quiany to start with the sequins and pipe cleaners and that I will be back shortly to help her with the glitter.

As soon as I'm able, I return to Mari's room and walk directly to Quiany. She notices me approaching and quickly hides the mask behind her back, then looks up at me sheepishly.

"What's going on, Quiany? You said you wanted to use some more glitter on your mask. Let's get to work on that."

"I used it already," she says quietly.

"Oh, really," I say, a question mark in my voice, not really sure how to handle this turn of events, "and where did you get the glitter from?"

"I went into your toolbox."

"Quiany," I say sternly, "you know that no one except me is ever allowed to go into my toolbox, for any reason."

"I know, Miss Miller," she says, sounding honestly upset despite her usual tough front, "but…"

"No buts about it, Quiany. No one. Not ever. For any reason."

For the moment, she buckles under. "Okay, Miss Miller."

I let some moments pass in silence. Then, "So… let's see it."

"Well," Quiany starts eagerly, "I know you always say less is more with glitter. But I used a little more than less…."

"Well, let me see it anyway, Quiany." My tone, I'm certain, conveys what I'm feeling, a mix of impatience and sympathy. Overall, I'm more than ready to be done with this, but somewhat surprise myself as I add, "Today is, after all, a special day. Maybe a little more than a little is okay, just for today." Nothing to be done about it now, I think. I might as well let her get out of this gracefully.

Reluctantly, she takes the mask out from behind her back and holds it out for me to see. She is right. She has definitely used a little more than a little. She has used so much, in fact, that the glitter covers all the work she had done the other day. All of the glitter colors, neatly separated in their little bottles in my toolbox, are all mixed together on her mask. None of the fabric of the mask shows through anywhere. The entire mask is glitter. Just glitter. And it is glorious.

I am at a loss for words, not sure of the appropriate teacher response to this. On the one hand, Quiany has broken several of our "art rules." On the other hand, she has created something very beautiful. To me, all of these things are important and I can't think quickly enough at the moment to determine which should have the priority.

"Quiany," I finally say, "you really did use a lot of glitter."

"Yes, Miss Miller, I know."

"And," I continue, "you do need to follow the rules. This is not the way we normally use glitter, nor can you go into my things without asking."

"I know, Miss Miller," she says, sounding quite miserable this time, and appearing to be on the verge of tears. "I know. I'm sorry. I won't do it again."

"But," I add slowly and cautiously, "your mask is very, very beautiful. Let me see it on you."

She keeps her head down and pulls the mask on, sliding the elastic of the mask up and over the black witch's hat. Taking a deep and exaggerated breath, Quiany picks her head up and looks straight at me. Her dark eyes peer anxiously from behind the magnificent mask. Her face, framed by the waves of her long, dark hair and the pointed, black hat, looks stunning. I know I will never forget how she looks at this moment.

I need to give this a lot more thought, I think to myself. Maybe less is not more all the time. Maybe Quiany, all the Quianys, know a lot more than I do about certain things.

Leaning down, not saying a word, I pull Quiany close, hugging the child she is now and the woman she will someday be.

~Celeste Miller

Echoes in the Classroom

The object of teaching a child is to enable
him to get along without his teacher.
~Elbert Hubbard

I sit here in this empty classroom in June,
desks cleared,
chairs stacked,
computers disassembled,
lamp wires wrapped like vines around
    their stands.
My grades are posted,
the checkout complete.
The cabinet doors are bare, naked without
    the student poems.
Only the photos of Earth,

Gandhi, Sojourner Truth, and Cesar
    Chavez remain
high above the windows
exempt from the maintenance list.
My pile of plants, poetry books, and
    journals
lie by the outside door, ready to return
    home for the summer.
The custodian and I are the only ones
left in the building.
I sit for a moment
in the stillness.
And from the carpet in the back,
up against the curtains,
a voice rises:

"Let every soldier hew him down a bough
And bear't before him..." (*Macbeth* 5.4.4-5)

And there, in the back of the room, I am certain I can see Matt, wielding his sword, cloaked in his cape, leading his army to defeat Macbeth and claim the kingdom as its rightful heir.

Matt, who had written to me in September, "I play football. I have a hard time presenting to the class. I have a hard time writing essays like getting started." Who revealed, "I need a little help writing an introduction. I would like to write my own poem." He shared that he "didn't read that good" and that his goals were "to finish a long book..." and "As a communicator my strengths are bad because I'm not that good at speaking to a big class. I think I would do better speaking to you."

Matt, who had sat with me in October, trying to find a focus for his memoir, looking for that significant moment in his trip to Mount Rushmore. Drawing the door that led out to the monument, the wooden walkway, the carvings, himself, his grandparents. Speaking from the picture to describe the size, the colors, the faces. Having the courage to return to his draft, to narrow his focus, to organize, to go small and detailed. He wrote that memoir, even though "at first I didn't even know what a memoir was." And he wrote poetry—an "I

Am From" poem, a found poem, a nonsense poem, poems he became willing to share in class. He wrote to the football coach to persuade him to purchase new jerseys for the JV team. He learned to be a writer. In fact, in November he wrote, "As a writer at this time, I just love it. I find writing fascinating to do."

He read *The Kite Runner* by choice, and "learned to understand what the book means in my eyes." He became comfortable in his small group to talk about the class readings: Atticus' courage, Langston Hughes' "salvation," Sandra Cisneros' disappointment. He explained, "At the beginning of the trimester I sucked in talking with groups…. I needed to break out of my shell and just be a communicator. Now I am a great communicator. I love speaking in groups, and to you, Mrs. Johnson.…"

So in February when were ready to study *Macbeth*, and we set the classroom up as a theater and Sarah brought in her collection of costumes and we pulled out our wooden swords and turned the lights down low, Matt said he wanted to take the role of Malcolm. Matt, who had been too shy to read his memoir in Author's Circle, wanted to take the role of Malcolm.

And so he became Malcolm. In our Readers' Theatre, he fled to England upon learning of the murder of his father; he urged Macduff to turn his own grief for his family's massacre to anger; he ordered his soldiers to hide themselves with boughs from Birnam Wood. Then just about the time we were nearing Act Five, Matt approached me after school, voice lowered, head bent, shoulders dropped, "Mrs. Johnson, my mother is taking me to Arizona to see my aunt next week. I'll be gone for five days." We both knew what his absence would mean: the class would finish the play without him. "I told my mother I'm Malcolm. I've read ahead and I know he's going to become king. I told her I want to be here to finish the play."

I commiserated with Matt that day, as disappointed as he that his culminating scene would pass to another student. I privately wondered if the confidence he had built might fade without the opportunity to perform his "finale." We brainstormed solutions like delaying the trip until Spring Break—but he had already tried that suggestion to no avail. I phoned his mother, but as friendly as the conversation was, she said she needed to keep her plans. Matt and I reluctantly accepted the reality and made lesson plans for his absence.

That Saturday, I saw Matt's grandmother in the checkout line at Safeway. She and I had known each other for more than twenty years—both of us educators. In fact, she had taught my son. I decided that fate must have given me this opportunity and joined her in line. After our initial, effusive hugs and hellos, I ventured my attempt."I'm sorry Matt will miss his performance in *Macbeth* next week."

"Oh, yes," she said, "he told me how much he loves being in that play."

"I sure was hoping his mother could put that trip off until Spring Break to give him a chance to claim the crown in the final scene. He was so excited about that moment."

"Hmm. Yes, I was thinking along those same lines," she agreed.

"Well, if you can use any of your grandma influence, it would be great for Matt."

That was that. She paid the cashier, we said our goodbyes, and I loaded my groceries onto the conveyor belt.

I arrive at school early—in the quiet of the morning—that's my best time to write plans on the board, score a few papers, check my e-mail, meet with struggling students. I had not scheduled appointments the next morning. But before the rush of the bus arrival, the flood of students in the hallway, Matt appeared at the classroom door. Smiling broadly, he strode across the floor. "Well, I've got some good news! My grandfather called my mother last night and talked her into taking our trip over Spring Break!"

"That's great news, Matt! You *are* Malcolm!" And then, with a bit of a whoop, we high-fived in celebration.

Matt readied for his final scene, nervous,

for he knew his lines closed the play. As Macduff entered with Macbeth's head, all shouted to Malcolm, "Hail King of Scotland!" Matt stood tall, cloaked in his cape, sword resting in triumph, Burger King crown now placed on his head. In his nervousness, he stumbled on a few of his phrases. Nevertheless, he did his best to proclaim:

> *...Of this dead butcher and his fiendlike queen,*
> *Who, as 'tis thought, by self and violent hands*
> *Took off her life—this and what needful else*
> *That calls upon us, by the grace of Grace*
> *We will perform in measure, time, and place:*
> *So thanks for all at once and to each one,*
> *Whom we invite to see us crowned at Scone.*
> (Macbeth 5.7.69-75)

With a final flourish, the stage emptied. Matt later chided himself for stumbling over those last words, but I assured him no one else had noticed. He had portrayed the noble role nobly and discovered the strength to perform in front of his peers.

Matt wants to perform in more plays; he wants to write more and read more. "What I learned is to just break out of your surrounding and just have fun while you're at school. My strengths are just to do it and not look back on your high school career and say hey I really wish I could have had fun in all of my classes."

So
as I sit here in this empty classroom,
I am certain I hear his voice,
see his broad smile,
feel the clap of his high-five celebration.
That's him
face-to-face with the antagonist,
rising to his challenge,
voicing his convictions,
and triumphing in his hope.

~*Susan Johnson*
2009 Washington State Teacher of the Year
English Language Arts teacher, grades 10–12

Real World Math

If you're going to be thinking,
you may as well think big.
~Donald Trump

It was my first year as a middle school math teacher, and in an effort to motivate and engage my students, I designed and implemented a classroom money system. Each day, students who came to class prepared earned a salary of twenty-five "royal" dollars. From the salary earned, the students paid monthly rent on their chairs and taxes on their classroom materials. My goals for the program were to help students learn the importance of financial management while also promoting positive classroom behavior.

I gave students daily opportunities to earn additional salary in the form of bonuses, such as ten dollars for catching my errors, fifty dollars for good mathematical arguments, and one hundred dollars for acing an assessment. Students deposited any money they earned in our class bank. As the banker, I maintained the accounts and notified students of dangerously low balances. After all, students knew what happened in the "real world" when you didn't have the money to pay rent, and none wanted to be evicted from his or her chair.

I explained that at the end of each quarter, after the students paid their rent, taxes and any fines, they could use discretionary money to bid on items in a class auction. Auction items varied from quarter to quarter, but typical fare included small trinkets, snacks, and school supplies.

My system worked beautifully. The students were fully engaged, especially when I began to distribute cash bonuses. I decided I could also minimize classroom disruptions if I levied fines. Students soon realized that use of inappropriate language or arriving tardy to class was not financially beneficial.

Three weeks into school Mayra met me at the door with a question.

"How much would it cost to buy my chair?"

"Buy your chair?"

"Well, if I could buy my chair, I won't have to pay you rent each month. Then I'll have more money to spend at the auction."

"That's really great thinking," I replied. "Let me think about it and I'll let you know."

I quickly calculated a reasonable purchase price and announced to the class, "If you prefer to save your money and purchase your chair, you can buy it for six hundred dollars."

Mayra's hand immediately shot up.

"So if I sit on the floor for twenty more days, I'll have enough money to buy my chair. Can I do that?"

Without fully processing the implications

of her plan, I responded, "Absolutely!"

She and several of her tablemates began to gather their materials and reposition themselves on the hard, wooden floor of our classroom. I thought to myself, "This will never last. They will be back in their chairs within a few minutes."

I certainly underestimated the resolve of middle school penny pinchers. Not only did Mayra and her crew last the hour, they resumed their positions the following day, with several peers joining in. By the end of the week, almost the entire class had selected seating on the floor. Each day, I stepped precariously over students to reach those who had questions. While it was slightly inconvenient for me, I reminded myself that these students were making a conscious decision to be frugal with their money.

The following Tuesday was Open House. Parent after parent flowed in to meet the teacher who was charging rent. They relayed stories of enthusiasm for the program from both their perspective and their child's.

"Thank you for teaching my child the value of money!" was a common refrain. I was now more motivated than ever to continue.

Two weeks later, Mayra arrived at my door announcing, "Today, I can buy my chair!"

I looked at the handwritten ledger she excitedly held. With no direction from me, she had recorded each deposit she had made to the bank. After verifying her accounting, I announced congratulations to her. She proudly took her "purchased" seat at her assigned table.

At the end of class, Mayra approached me with another question, "Now, can I save more money and buy José's chair, and then charge him higher rent?"

I laughed. Clearly, my goal of improving financial management had been met by at least one of my students and I'm sure those skills will serve her well in the future.

~Heather Sparks
2009 Oklahoma State Teacher of the Year
Algebra, Pre-Algebra teacher, grade 8

Field Trip Fiasco

Every day may not be good,
but there's something good in every day.
~Author Unknown

When I accepted the teaching position at the small private school in the Green Mountains of Vermont, I expected to be passing on my love of language to middle-school children with learning disabilities. I did not expect to be standing in a parking lot with a bleeding little girl surrounded by Vermont state troopers, hands at their holsters. But that was exactly my position at 11:25 AM one August day.

At seven years old, Sabrina was on her third set of adoptive parents when she showed up at

Autumn Acres. Our little school only housed about sixty kids, but they were sixty kids who'd already seen more horrible things than most people ever see. Sabrina had it worst of all.

I wasn't with them at recess when it happened, but Sabrina managed to climb fifteen feet up a tree and then fall. When I came into work Monday morning, teachers huddled in corners, from which I could hear snatches of conversation: "... wasn't being watched... shouldn't be left alone... bit her tongue completely in half...."

Sabrina showed up for school on Friday with her jaw wired shut. They were able to re-attach the tongue, but there had been significant nerve damage, and it was questionable that she'd ever be able to speak normally again. Mr. Garrity, the principal, pulled me aside as I was warming up the van to take the kids on a field trip.

"Mr. Kaiser, we really want to get Sabrina reintegrated into the population as quickly as possible."

"Sabrina? I don't know if bringing her is a

good idea. We'll be walking a couple of miles. If something should happen…"

"Look, Mr. Kaiser. Rather than punish her even more, I'd like you to take her along on the field trip today."

Of course they wanted Sabrina to go on the field trip. That way none of the administrators would have to deal with her back at the school.

I parked the raucous student-packed van in the handicapped spot at the Green Mountain Animal Sanctuary. Mrs. Bourne, the science teacher, got out of the van, and opened the back door to let the kids out to stretch their legs and eat the orange slices we'd brought for snack. The seven other teachers walked over with their lists. Each teacher would have eight students.

I heard a cough behind me, and there sat Sabrina alone in the van. I looked at my clipboard; she was not mine. Her blue eyes looked even bigger than usual, her face drawn and her jaw sticking out as if she was angry. I couldn't tell if she truly was, or if the wiring made her look so. I stepped into the van and extended my hand to her, and her big eyes became narrow slits. She shook her head vigorously. She didn't know me. To someone who'd experienced terrible things at the hands of those closest to her, a stranger must have looked like another predator. I stepped back and Sabrina extended a white, skinny arm to Mrs. Bourne.

Mrs. Bourne took her group straight to the skunk pen, outside of which was a table holding little metal cans. Each can had a perforated top, and everyone was invited to pick up a can and smell the skunk's musk. The badger pen was located near the skunk pen and the badger musk smelled like the worst armpit in the world according to one boy. He was right. I gagged after I lifted the can to my nose.

We continued on the winding tarmac to the hut housing the moles. When I stepped through the doorway I saw Sabrina standing perfectly still and staring up at a mole burrow behind the glass. Behind her was what looked like a giant captain's wheel, but with badgers and moles and skunks and mountain lions and other animals painted on it. When the wheel stopped, the animals would be lined up with either what they preyed on, or what preyed on them. But it was the wheel itself that preyed on little Sabrina, because when she took a step back, the wheel's wooden handle slammed right down on top of her head. She collapsed to her knees and I heard the haunting, muted cry of a child trying to scream through a wired jaw. Sabrina's lips were drawn back as far as they would go and her teeth were bared to expose the thin strips of metal running across her teeth, and blood seeped from between her teeth. She'd bitten her tongue stitches.

I radioed for help, and fearing she might choke on her blood, I stooped and in one motion tipped her over into my arms and stood. She immediately began kicking her feet wildly and thrashing and screaming as if she had a gag in her mouth. I began running the mile or so back to the van.

Sabrina was still kicking as I ran, and her

attempts at screaming had jetted blood from between her teeth all over the right side of my head and face. Sabrina was only sixty pounds, but she began to get heavy as I plodded along, fetching strange looks from bystanders who saw a man running away with a screaming, bloody girl who sounded as if she'd been gagged.

The science teacher Catharine had heard my radio transmission and she was waiting at the van, with a little boy named Derek.

She said, "Do you want me to drive her to the hospital?"

"I can drive her. Can you just get her in the van for me? She doesn't trust me." I put Sabrina down and Catharine took both her hands and bent down, whispered something to her. Surprisingly, Sabrina stepped into the van and sat in the very back. Derek climbed in and even snapped her seatbelt on, then belted himself in too.

"Can I come?"

"Oh, um, actually that's not a bad idea, Derek." I started the van and heard movement behind me—Sabrina was trying to unbuckle her seatbelt, and Derek was holding her hands so she couldn't.

"Hip-hop!" cried Derek. "She likes hip-hop!" I tuned the radio to a rap station.

"Turn it up! Loud!" he cried. In the rearview mirror, I could see Sabrina smiling in her blood-sprayed white T-shirt, bouncing to the rhythm.

I called the school on my way to the hospital, but they gave me other instructions. Sabrina's parents did not want her brought to the small local hospital, but to Children's Hospital Boston, where she had her tongue sewed back on in the first place. I started to protest, but she did seem okay back there with Derek, so I agreed to meet Sabrina's parents in a parking lot on Main Street.

And it was there, with hip-hop music blasting, blood-covered Sabrina and Derek dancing, leaning against the driver's door myself covered with blood, that the three Vermont state police cruisers arrived and surrounded me.

They exited their vehicles and, gun hands at their hips, slowly began walking toward me. I was leaning on the car watching this unfold, thinking this was just what I needed to top off this wonderful day

"I've got a hurt kid here—I'm waiting for her parents to pick her up!" I yelled. They closed in, and I handed over my license. They seemed to think they'd caught me at something. Then I saw an older woman standing on her porch, peeking out from behind a post with a cordless phone in her hand. Of course I would probably have thought it suspicious too if I saw a man in his late twenties hanging out with a bloody little girl, having a hip-hop dance party in a parking lot. As it turned out, they thought I was a pedophile luring children with music.

When I look back at that day, my most stressful ever of teaching, what sticks in my mind is not being mistaken for a pedophile, or any animosity toward poor wounded Sabrina, but the kindness of that little boy Derek, who like so many good people who pass briefly through our lives, touched me with his good-will and moved on before I let him know how grateful I was.

~Ron Kaiser, Jr.

Full of Surprises

Every survival kit should include a sense of humor.
~Author Unknown

After receiving a staff e-mail containing pictures of outlandish things that kids do, I felt compelled to share with my fellow second grade teachers my own story of a student who could have easily been in many of those pictures. My first year teaching I thought my school administration was out to get me. As an inexperienced teacher, every child of a staff member who was in second grade was placed in my class. No pressure there, right? To add to that, I also taught five Spanish speaking students and I had not yet received my bilingual certification. At this point, my confidence level as a new teacher had declined tremendously. As unnerved as I was throughout my initial teaching experience, the year went by with minimal complications. Little did I know my second year of teaching would be filled with prolific challenges.

Let's call her Meredith.... Meredith was a beautiful child who could light up a room with her laughter and smile. She had a fantastic sense of humor and brought a great deal of joy to our classroom. However, Meredith had a tendency to find herself in unusual situations. Take the head stuck in the chair incident. How this happened, I have no idea. As I was at the chalkboard displaying new vocabulary words, Meredith somehow managed to wedge her head in an opening in the back of the chair. Lesson number one—do not turn your back on them for one second.

We abruptly discontinued our vocabulary lesson so that I could attempt to remove Meredith's head from its unexpected position.

Meredith twisted and turned, stretched and pulled to no avail. As she began to cry, I thought her tears might provide some lubrication to help slide her head back through the opening. When that theory proved to be ineffective, I proceeded to call our head custodian. He came over right away armed with his tools and his sense of humor. He then attempted to have Meredith twist and turn, and stretch and pull. Once again... nothing. As a last resort, the custodian removed the back of the chair from its supporting pieces and Meredith was freed from her confinement. It did not take long for Meredith's tears to turn to impish laughter and we were able to continue with our day. Please note I did not schedule for a removal of head from chair in my lesson plans.

This was the incident that first came to mind after receiving the entertaining images of curious child behavior. But this is not my only story involving Meredith and her mischievous manner. Another vivid memory I have of that year involved measuring tape, students jumping and me flat on the floor. As part of a measurement activity, students jumped as far as they could and we measured the distance. We did this activity one student at a time with me on one end of the tape measure and one student on the other end. I asked students who were waiting for their turn or who had already finished to sit in a separate area and observe. As I moved forward and backward, and up and down, I trusted that I could do so safely. Lesson number two—do not have false confidence in your own physical wellbeing in the classroom.

As I blindly backed away from a student to measure a jump, I encountered an obstacle and fell to the floor. Through my legs in the air, there sat Meredith, scrunched in a ball on the floor in front of me. I couldn't decide if I wanted to laugh or shout. After briefly sharing a laugh with my students, I instructed them one more time regarding what should occur during this activity and stressed the importance of listening and following directions in order to maintain a safe classroom environment.

As I shared these stories with my colleagues who had just received the exuberant e-mail that triggered my memory, an innocent, inexperienced student teacher gasped in horror and said, "That's the kind of thing I'm afraid of!" I smiled at her and said, "Don't be afraid of these types of things. They're the kind of things that keep it interesting." As I thought about my response to her, I realized that my biggest disasters are some of my best memories. I learned that even the best plans can and will be interrupted by heads stuck in chairs and teachers crashing to the floor. And my memories of Meredith... she will forever brighten my day and bring me back to reality.

~Blythe Turner
2009 New Mexico State Teacher of the Year
Bilingual teacher, grade 2

The Gift of Self-Esteem

To free us from the expectations of others, to give
us back to ourselves—there lies the great,
singular power of self-respect.
~Joan Didion

I remember the day. I was in Senior English, two weeks away from high school graduation. I lived two lives: one as an under-achiever in the classroom and the other as the esteemed at-home tutor who helped my younger brother overcome the obstacles of learning with Attention Deficit Disorder. I wrote really bad raps to help him memorize those mundane history facts he would be required to regurgitate on a test. I used a picture of a hamburger to teach him the layers of writing an essay. I filmed plays in which I also took a role, hoping he would feel a sense of personal achievement. In short, I was more challenged and motivated by tutoring my brother than I was by my own studies or any teacher in school. My parents knew me as creative and talented but my teachers only knew me as a classic underachiever.

The epiphany came that day in Senior English. We had finished our work early, and bursting with my news, I walked up to my teacher's desk and stood watching her enter grades in her grade book. I waited for an acknowledgement. Getting none, I started, "I know what I want to do."

She didn't look up, but kept entering final grades. "Yes, Leanne, what is it you want to do?

"I want to teach!" I exclaimed, full of pride and purpose. Her pen came to a dead halt as she slowly removed her eyeglasses and looked up at me standing eagerly over her desk. She saw a 2.3 GPA standing in front of her with dreams that seemed to contradict that reality. She saw a shy, aimless young lady who seemed more interested in social aspirations than anything academic. She saw failure and indifference to success.

"Really," she retorted. It was not a question, but a comment. I nodded, waiting anxiously for her confirmation and encouragement. It didn't come. Instead, she advised, "You might want to rethink that decision because I'm just not sure you are college material." I digested that for a moment, waiting for anything else she might add, but nothing came. She stared at me as if I was supposed to digest those words of wisdom thoughtfully, so I sat back down, allowing her perception of me to define my potential and future.

That day I told my parents I would not be going to college. Luckily, my parents told *me* differently. Four years later, I graduated from one of the top three schools in education within the United States, at the time, and received a double major in Secondary English Education and Communications and Theater Arts.

I still remember that high school teacher and the effect she had on my self-esteem. With that personal experience, my mission statement is squarely mounted on my classroom door that, among other goals, highlights my purpose of "raising my students' self-esteem through personal achievement." Research and education journals agree with this ambitious goal, but ultimately the proof came for me on the day I was called to the principal's office. "Shut the door," she commanded. In my career, that sentence has never proved to have a positive outcome. Having taught at-risk students for several years, I wasn't sure if I was going to hear about some tragedy involving a student, or some personal reprimand; either way, I knew it was not going to be good news.

She began with an unexpected question. "Do you remember when you had some things stolen from your classroom a few years ago?"

I did remember reporting several items missing from my closet. Important things like Little Debbie Swiss Cake Rolls, oatmeal cookies, moon pies, and Fruit Roll-Ups. Oh yes, and those caramels with the white crème in them that tastes like Christmas. These "important" things in my closet served as sanity snacks for my own children when the bus from the elementary and primary school dropped them off at the high school where I worked. My girls would go straight to the closet, get a snack, and start their homework. We had a routine that allowed me to get some work done before heading home for the day.

I remembered one day leaving my room for a few minutes during my planning period to run errands around campus, and when I came back all of the freshly stocked goodies were gone, boxes and all. I had reported the theft to the resource officer, but I had never heard any more about it. "Yes," I said, confused and curious. "I remember. Why?"

"Well, I am only telling you this now

because the student has graduated, and I thought you should know the impact you are having on the lives of your students." She told me who had stolen those items—a boy in my English class who had little to no support at home, but had the heart of a champion and potential that I wanted him to see through my eyes. "Well," she continued, "we rolled back the tapes to see who had entered your room around the timeframe in question, and we saw him. We called him to the office, and he admitted it right away. When the school officer asked him if he had anything else he wanted to say, he said, 'I have one request. Please don't tell Ms. Maule because she's the only one who believes in me.'"

I sat there in her office welling up with tears at this story of a young man who was one of my biggest fans, showed such great potential, and was the "Rock" for me when I was absent, helping to keep others on task. He had me for the first time in three rounds of fresh-man English. I remember the day I saw him graduate and took my picture with him under the lights on the football field.

"I wanted you to know the truth, and I hope you understand why I waited to tell you for so long," she continued.

"Thank you, Mrs. Kellogg. Thank you," I said, leaving her office with the validation I so desperately wished I had from my Senior English teacher years before.

Yes, I teach to enhance student learning. Ultimately, however, I want my students to experience empowerment and self-esteem from personal achievement. When my seniors graduate, I share a quote from Henry David Thoreau: "Most men lead lives of quiet desperation and go to the grave with the song still in them." I challenge them to NOT be "most" men. I toast them as they continue their journey to find their heart's song as I have found mine. I tell them, "No money in the world can buy the feeling of waking up every day and doing a job you love that uses your talents in a challenging way. Find it and sing it." I could

not wish a more precious gift for them than
this.

~Leanne Maule-Sims
2009 Georgia State Teacher of the Year
English, British Literature teacher, grade 12

A Teacher's Influence

The mediocre teacher tells. The good teacher explains.
The superior teacher demonstrates.
The great teacher inspires.
~William Arthur Ward

My experiences this past year as Nebraska State Teacher of the Year have prompted me to give much thought to why I became a teacher. My parents were my greatest supporters when I decided I wanted to become a teacher as a senior in high school. There were also a few teachers who encouraged me without even knowing it. I decided to locate Mr. Eloe, my junior high Industrial Arts teacher, to let him know what his teaching and his class meant to me.

I located Mr. Eloe in another state and left him a message. One Sunday evening a few weeks later, I answered the phone and immediately recognized a voice that I had not heard in over forty years. Mr. Eloe began with, "Hello Dan, how should I know you?" I explained to him who I was and told him he had taught me.

Mr. Eloe had instructed us in forming a company, guided us in coming up with a product (The Doll Fly), helped us to learn how to advertise, assisted us in purchasing our shares of stock, constructed an assembly line, and guided us in selling our products. Mr. Eloe told me that he had attended a summer workshop entitled "Innovative Approaches to Teaching Industrial Arts" and tried it out on us that school year. I still had three of my doll flies; however, they were too valuable to use fishing. I told Mr. Eloe that the doll fly unit was instrumental in leading me to a thirty-five year teaching career.

In reflecting, I can easily remember those students who I know I had an impact on throughout my teaching career, but now I think of all those students that I maybe had an impact on without realizing it. I only hope that I have been able to instill a passion for industrial technology education and for learning as was done for me by Mr. Eloe, even though he didn't remember me.

One student who I know I helped, and whose name I still remember, was Bob. In the summer of 1976, I took a teaching job in a high school system with an enrollment of close to 1,000 students. I had taught just one year prior to this in a high school of approximately 150 students. So being a little anxious, I talked to some of the veteran teachers in my department about my class rosters. They looked at my student lists and when they arrived at Bob's name there was a huge pause. Bob had gotten into serious trouble at the junior high school.

Throughout the first quarter in our class, I covered the various machines used in a woodworking shop by giving lectures, machine demonstrations, and safety tests to determine who would be allowed to use the machines. Because of the modular schedule our school was using, seven days would pass between my lecture and the machine safety test. Bob received scores in the teens on the first couple of tests. As I went over the tests in the class, I could see anger and disappointment building in Bob because of another failing grade. He wanted to use the machines and knew these tests were keeping him away from what he had enrolled in the class to do.

I called Bob in after class one day to talk to him about his low scores and to see what we could do together to improve his testing. I learned he had some definite chips on his shoulder because of earlier failures in his education. I tried reviewing with Bob individually before the next test, but he received the same results. So, Bob and I had another talk about giving me his best effort. I asked Bob what I could do to help. Bob replied, "Nothing." For a freshman, Bob was tall and physically developed beyond his age, but that day I learned

Bob had trouble even reading a comic book.

I was finally able to talk Bob into going down to the reading teacher with me so the three of us could develop a plan to help him with his work. For the next machine test, Bob agreed to go to the reading teacher's room so she could read the test questions and record his responses. Bob scored an 85% on most tests after this and he was able to do this by just listening, because he would rarely take notes.

Bob and I developed a good working relationship and I seldom saw his angry side. Bob completed the required project and found a passion for using the woodworking lathe. On the lathe, he was able to turn his wood into bowls and took pride in making them for his mom, sisters, and aunts.

I stopped worrying about keeping my eye on Bob during lab. My only problem was to get him out of the woodworking shop and on to his next class. He preferred to keep working in the woods lab. One day Bob came into class to find me upset because someone had lost one of my lathe parts, which made it inoperable. Bob looked at me and without hesitation said, "Mr. McCarthy I know where your part went. I am not a stool pigeon and I won't tell you who threw your part out the window, but your part is out there in the snow bank."

I asked, "Bob, would you mind going out to get it for me?" He went right out and found the part and returned it to me.

I know that Bob has not always had an easy life since he left high school. Recently, I ran into Bob at a convenience store. It has now been some thirty years since Bob was in my class. He looked at me and said, "You don't know who I am, do you?"

I said, "Sure I do. How are you doing, Bob? It has been a long time since I have seen you, so what have you been up to?" The biggest smile came across his face when he realized that I remembered him. We continued catching up with what each of us had been doing. I learned many of the bowls he had turned were still being cherished and used by his relatives today. Bob went on to express how amazed he was that I was still teaching. It was so good to learn he had his life on track and had a good position with a local concrete contractor.

Thanks to Bob, I learned very early in my teaching career that not all teachers relate the same to all students and not all students relate the same to all teachers. Without knowing it, Bob taught me that it is important to allow students the opportunity to show whether they can or cannot be trusted. With Bob's help, I learned to form my opinions about my students based on their behavior and performance within my classroom rather than by listening to opinions of others based on their experiences and perceptions.

~Dan McCarthy
2009 Nebraska State Teacher of the Year
Industrial Technology teacher, grades 9–12

A Lesson in Friendship

A teacher is one who makes himself
progressively unnecessary.
~Thomas Carruthers

It is difficult to believe that I won't be getting a card from Mrs. Hanson at Christmas this year—or any more birthday cards filled with glitter hearts or multicolored, balloon-shaped confetti. For almost twenty years I looked forward to receiving a greeting or a handwritten letter from my fourth grade teacher, and I really thought she might come to my wedding even though we hadn't seen each other in sixteen years, since my family moved from

Horsham, Pennsylvania to a rural town almost five hours away.

• • •

When homeroom assignments came out in the summer of 1989, I was petrified and immediately wanted my room changed. As a third grader passing Mrs. Hanson's classroom at Round Meadow Elementary School, I'd occasionally heard her voice coming from her classroom doorway when she raised it above the noise of her students instructing them to "pay attention." I knew she probably yelled, and I was sure that fourth grade was destined to be a year I would never forget. I was right.

I dreaded the start of school. I had new glasses that I hated. Big and round and pink and blue, they took up most of my face and magnified my cheekbones. Nearly all of my friends had gotten braces over the summer. My teeth were still crooked. While some of the other more popular girls in my class were starting to experiment with purple eye shadow and mascara, I went without any. Just plain Julie Mellott. No pierced ears. Mousy brown, unstyled hair. And giant glasses.

Mrs. Hanson was a sixty-year-old, slender woman with her hair dyed a light reddish brown and styled on the top of her head. Eventually, I learned that Mrs. Hanson didn't yell, but she kept order in her classroom and encouraged respect. While some of my classmates called her "hard," I really liked the challenge that having her for a teacher presented. And she was always nice to me. She showed compassion toward me when others teased me on the playground and when I learned my grandmother was very sick. She even nominated me to speak in front of the senior class about the dangers of drinking and driving. I loved Mrs. Hanson and I loved fourth grade.

I still stopped in to visit Mrs. Hanson after moving on through school, and she became my pen pal at her suggestion. Since I was moving away and she was retiring, Mrs. Hanson thought it would be nice if we kept in touch with each other. Over the years I continued to send her letters and pictures—sharing my success stories and my firsts. She would tell me about her travels and visits with family. I always looked forward to a lengthy letter each summer. She always called me her "special girl."

After graduating from college and living on my own for a few years, I took a job in Boston and lost touch with Mrs. Hanson for a few months. Settling in to a new job, a new apartment and a new lifestyle took up most of my time. The first opportunity I had to reach out to Mrs. Hanson was over the holidays.

Days later, I received a card in return:

...Wishing you peace,
and wishing you love.
Merry Christmas!
With much love,
Mrs. Hanson

We never lost touch again.

Recently, I received a voicemail from Greg Hanson. Although we had never spoken before, I sensed that he knew me already. "I'm Janice Hanson's son. Mom is in a hospice," he explained. "She's asked me to contact you—she would like you to call. We've been hearing all about you for years." Tears filled my eyes because I knew a hospice could only mean one thing, and I had to prepare myself mentally and emotionally to contact my teacher for what might be the last time. "She's having a good day, and you are on her top-ten list, if you want to call it that. We're keeping her comfortable and you are one of the people she wants to know that she is here."

I hadn't talked to Mrs. Hanson in nearly a year. The last time we had spoken, I called to tell her about my engagement. I couldn't wait to share my excitement with my oldest friend. The news of her suffering from chronic obstructive pulmonary disease (COPD) was rather surprising, because in all of our conversations, all of our letters, Mrs. Hanson had never let on that she wasn't feeling well. After several hours of trying to collect my emotions and to talk without crying, I picked up the phone and dialed her hospice.

I will never forget the seven minutes that I spent on the phone with Mrs. Hanson. It was so easy not to cry because it seemed like nothing had ever changed. Although she was a little more difficult to understand and I could hear the sound of her oxygen in the background, her voice was the same, her laugh was the same, and her memory was so clear. "So how was your second winter in Boston? I bet you got a lot of snow. Do you like your job? What are you doing now? I've always been so proud of you. Thank you for sending the ivy plant. It's a nice gift to remind me of a special girl."

I could tell that it was getting more difficult for her to talk, and she wrapped up the call, "Well, I'll let you go. But if someone would ever get me some paper around here, I would write you a letter. Maybe I'll call you sometime."

My mind was spinning because I knew our conversation was ending. How could I say goodbye to an important part of my life for twenty years—for more than half my lifetime? "You are a very special part of my life," I started. "I'm so happy that we've kept in touch over the years. I love you."

"I love you, too," she said.

Mrs. Hanson passed away in her sleep two weeks later.

I wish I could say that I remember the first day of school or the first lesson that Mrs. Hanson taught to me, but I can't. What made Mrs. Hanson a special teacher to me was not what I learned in her classroom. It's not the books that she read to us or the facts that she taught. Mrs. Hanson inspired me in so many ways. I learned to be kinder and more compassionate. I aspired to make a difference in the lives of others. But more than anything she could have instructed from a text book, Mrs. Hanson taught me a lesson in friendship. I learned it can span generation gaps, twenty years and 300 miles. I learned friendship lives forever.

~Julie Mellott George

Making a Difference

*Don't judge each day by the harvest
you reap but by the seeds that you plant.*
~Robert Louis Stevenson

Reflecting on more than two decades of teaching is not as easy as it may sound. My experiences have been many, the students diverse, the days long, my patience tested, but my endurance strong. You see, I always promised myself that I wouldn't just do something to "do it." I wouldn't just occupy a desk, office, or classroom for the goal of punching in and punching out. My goal was to wake up in the morning with a purpose, spend my days helping children understand, and fall asleep knowing that I made a difference. It was a good goal... noble, respectable, and simple.

I've never been confused about my purpose and I thoroughly enjoy being involved with a child's learning and understanding. However, have I achieved my goal? Do I fall asleep every night knowing that I made a difference that day? Humbly, the answer is no. As a matter of fact, the days spent hoping that I am making a difference far outnumber the days of knowing.

Living in a small agricultural community in Iowa, I am surrounded by cornfields, bean fields... and more cornfields! The farmers often talk about seed, time, and harvest. They always know what to sow, when to sow it, and where to sow the seed. I witness the farmers planting seed with a work ethic and fervor that instantly gains my admiration. They cannot afford to focus on anything other than sowing seed!

Once the seed is in the ground, with absolutely no evidence of a single plant in the field, the farmers begin watering and fertilizing that which was sown. They invest countless hours providing for and protecting their unseen crop. They realize that time is an essential ingredient in producing what they desire. The expectation is high, regardless of what they have seen up to that point. After a while, the crops are fully grown. The farmers get to harvest the fields, and see the result of their labor. They no longer wonder if the work was worth it… they know that it was!

There are days when I come to school with important decisions, deadlines, family issues, lack of sleep, etc. taking priority in my mind. I look at the lesson plans prepared for that day, knowing that I could easily hit the Auto-Pilot button, coast through the day, and pass the time until I could attend to more "important" matters. I glance up at my class and notice several elementary-aged children with similar concerns. They are also coming to school with important decisions, deadlines, family issues, lack of sleep, etc. They want to hit the auto-pilot button worse than I do!

I have had to pause and ask myself, "What could possibly be more important than watering and fertilizing these precious seeds?" I am happiest when I am reminded of this fact, and understand that a difference will be made regardless of the evidence that is shown that day.

I've sown seeds impacting the lives of hundreds of students over the years. I do my best to stay in touch with my former students, hoping to get a glimpse of the harvest that I've sown. I hope I have made a difference to all of my students, but I know I have made a difference to some. They've expressed that to me in a variety of ways. At times, former students come back to my classroom to show me their report cards, just come to talk, or bring me schedules of the extracurricular activities they are involved in. However, I will never forget the day I received a specific letter from a former student.

This letter came at the perfect time. I had just spent several days hoping that I was making a difference, seeing little to no results in my classroom. I still have the letter and look at it often. It reads:

> *Dear Ms. H:*
>
> *You were my teacher in fourth and fifth grade. I still remember the lessons that I learned in your class to this day. I remember how I used to sit in my seat and complain about certain math problems and how I'd never learn how to do them. You insisted that with your help and lots of effort on my part I would understand. You were right. You taught me that it is important to work hard and try because nothing is impossible to learn or do.*
>
> *You have been there for me on countless occasions with both academic and personal issues. For example, you were willing to listen and help me when I was having a hard time dealing with my parents' divorce. You became someone I look up to, trust, and admire. You always said that we were your*

children because you didn't have any of your own. I know you truly care for all of us this way.

So, for always being there for me in the good times and the bad, I want to thank you and let you know that you will always have a very special place in my heart.

A teacher's commitment never begins and ends with the first and last bell of the day. A teacher's thoughts never remain in the school buildings overnight. A teacher's love for his or her students never fades at the end of the school year. A teacher's greatest reward is impacting lives, knowing that a difference has been made.

~Linda Heffner
2009 Iowa State Teacher of the Year
Elementary teacher, grade 4

Special Treatment

We are all special cases.
~Albert Camus

Kayla sat in the back of my classroom. She usually had a rather dazed look about her, as though she'd just narrowly missed being hit by a bus. When I tried to engage her, she was always polite and respectful. She never broke any rules. However, I had a hard time determining her academic potential. She wasn't failing, but I had a sense that she was capable of more than the "C's" and "B's" she earned.

"How was your weekend?" I asked her one Monday morning.

Her rote response, "Fine," greeted my ears uncertainly.

"Is everything okay?" I asked. She seemed more dazed than usual.

Kayla shook her head and then nodded. "My brother was home for the weekend."

There was nothing in my file about her family situation. I mentioned her to a colleague who had taught her the previous year.

"Poor kid," she said. "Has two siblings with autism. One of them had to be institution-alized. Guess he comes home sometimes."

That explained a great deal about Kayla's behavior. She tiptoed past students, always on alert that one might do something unexpected.

"The kid was so shell shocked that at one point the parents thought she might have some sort of disability as well."

"I wish someone had told me this at the beginning of the year."

"Sorry," my colleague replied. "I went through the same thing last year. Should have given you a heads up."

Returning to my classroom with a new understanding, as well as a plan to look up more about autism, I saw Kayla at the lunch tables with a woman who looked vaguely familiar. She wasn't on staff at the school. Perhaps I'd met her at back-to-school night.

"How was lunch?" I asked her. "Was that your mother?" Most middle school children would have died of embarrassment at the thought of a parent showing up to have lunch with them.

Kayla smiled. "Yeah. She has lunch with me sometimes, when she can get away."

"What a nice treat," I responded.

"It is nice, and calm and quiet. The only time Mom and I can talk."

Suddenly I understood. "Must be hard at home with your brothers."

"Well, my parents work really hard and they try to find ways to give me attention, too. But I understand."

At that moment, Kayla seemed to me so mature for her age. She didn't care what any students thought about having lunch with her mother at school. She stole moments wherever she could find them.

I would never completely understand what life was like for her at home. Some days were better than others; I could always tell by looking in Kayla's eyes.

In fact, she shuffled in the day of an important test looking like she could use a good night's sleep.

"Kayla?" I began, but she interrupted, nearly in tears.

"I couldn't... I didn't... the test...."

"Bad night?" I asked without need for elaboration.

Kayla simply nodded.

I wrote a note on the health slip. "Here. Why don't you go lie down in the nurse's office until next period. You can take the test tomorrow."

The girl looked confused, grateful, and hesitant all at once. "I... I don't want any special treatment."

"Kayla, we are all special. And everyone needs a little special treatment from time to time."

~D. B. Zane

Meet Our Contributors

Julie Mellott George graduated magna cum laude from Penn State Altoona with a Bachelor of Arts degree in English. She works as an assistant director of marketing for college admission in Boston. Julie enjoys reading, writing and traveling with her new husband.

Linda Heffner (Iowa STOY) completed undergraduate studies at Briar Cliff University in Sioux City, IA. She received her Masters in Administration from Wayne State College. Linda began teaching in 1984 at Everett Elementary School in Sioux City, IA. She still teaches at Everett today. Linda enjoys hiking, athletics, and time with family.

Susan Johnson (Washington STOY) teaches high school English Language Arts in the Cascade

Mountains. She is also a Co-Director of the Central Washington Writing Project. Her love of language and literacy drives her teaching as well as her writing.

Ronald W. Kaiser, Jr. received his Master's degree in English Literature from the University of New Hampshire. He lives and teaches English in New Hampshire's Lakes Region. Writing stories is his second passion, next to his radiant wife. And then of course there are his two terriers.

Leanne Maule-Sims (Georgia STOY), now an educator in North Georgia, earned her Bachelor's degree in English Education from Eastern Michigan University. Her Master's degree is in Technology and her Specialist Degree, from Nova Southeastern University, is in Brain-based Learning. She plans to write books on the art and science of motivating students.

Dan McCarthy (Nebraska STOY) received his BA (1975) and MS in Education (1983) from Kearney

State College. He has devoted his thirty-five-year career to teaching mechanical and architectural drafting at Hastings Senior High School. He met his wife during their first year of teaching and they have three grown children. E-mail Dan at dmccarth@esu9.org.

Celeste M. Miller, a New York City public school teacher, is a Learning Specialist at the Professional Performing Arts School in Manhattan. Following a corporate career, she became a New York City Teaching Fellow, teaching art to students with special needs and earning a Master's degree in Education before joining the staff of PPAS. E-mail her at Celeste17@juno.com.

Adrienne C. Reynolds was a teacher for twenty-two years and now works for Broward County Schools as a Testing Specialist. Adrienne enjoys being with her family and volunteering. One of the goals on her "bucket list" is to write a book that will inspire others for generations to come. Please e-mail her at clasywritr@bellsouth.net.

Heather Sparks (Oklahoma STOY) received her BS and Master of Education, with honors, from Oklahoma City University in 1995. She teaches sixth and eighth graders at Taft Middle School in Oklahoma City. Heather is the 2008 recipient of the Presidential Award for Excellence in Mathematics Teaching. Visit her website: www.hisparks.com.

Blythe Turner (New Mexico STOY) received her Bachelor of Education and Master of Education at Eastern New Mexico University. She is a second grade bilingual teacher and is currently a doctoral student in the Language, Literacy and Socio-Cultural Studies department at the University of New Mexico.

D. B. Zane has a multiple-subject credential as well as a single-subject credential in social studies. She currently works for the Middle School Parliamentary Debate Program. In her spare time, she enjoys reading and writing.

Meet Our Authors

Jack Canfield is the co-creator of the *Chicken Soup for the Soul* series, which *Time* magazine has called "the publishing phenomenon of the decade." Jack is also the coauthor of many other bestselling books.

Jack is the CEO of the Canfield Training Group in Santa Barbara, California, and founder of the Foundation for Self-Esteem in Culver City, California. He has conducted intensive personal and professional development seminars on the principles of success for more than a million people in twenty-three countries, has spoken to hundreds of thousands of people at more than 1,000 corporations, universities, professional conferences and conventions, and has been seen by millions more on national television shows.

Jack has received many awards and honors, including three honorary doctorates and a Guinness World Records Certificate for having seven books from the *Chicken Soup for the Soul* series appearing on the New York Times bestseller list on May 24, 1998.

You can reach Jack at
www.jackcanfield.com.

Mark Victor Hansen is the co-founder of Chicken Soup for the Soul, along with Jack Canfield. He is a sought-after keynote speaker, bestselling author, and marketing maven. Mark's powerful messages of possibility, opportunity, and action have created powerful change in thousands of organizations and millions of individuals worldwide.

Mark is a prolific writer with many bestselling books in addition to the *Chicken Soup for the Soul* series. Mark has had a profound influence in the field of human potential through his library of audios, videos, and articles in the areas of big thinking, sales achievement, wealth building, publishing success, and personal and professional development. He is also the founder of the MEGA Seminar Series.

Mark has received numerous awards that honor his entrepreneurial spirit, philanthropic heart, and business acumen. He is a lifetime member of the Horatio Alger Association of Distinguished Americans.

You can reach Mark at
www.markvictorhansen.com.

Amy Newmark is Chicken Soup for the Soul's publisher and editor-in-chief, after a thirty-year career as a writer, speaker, financial analyst, and business executive in the worlds of finance and telecommunications. Amy is a *magna cum laude* graduate of Harvard College, where she majored in Portuguese, minored in French, and traveled extensively. She and her husband have four grown children.

After a long career writing books on telecommunications, voluminous financial reports, business plans, and corporate press releases, Chicken

Soup for the Soul is a breath of fresh air for Amy. She has fallen in love with Chicken Soup for the Soul and its life-changing books, and really enjoys putting these books together for Chicken Soup for the Soul's wonderful readers. She has coauthored more than five dozen *Chicken Soup for the Soul* books and has edited another three dozen.

You can reach Amy with any questions or comments through webmaster@chickensoupforthe-soul.com and you can follow her on Twitter @amynewmark or @chickensoupsoul.

Chicken Soup for the Soul
Improving Your Life Every Day

Real people sharing real stories—for fifteen years. Now, Chicken Soup for the Soul has gone beyond the bookstore to become a world leader in life improvement. Through books, movies, DVDs, online resources and other partnerships, we bring hope, courage, inspiration and love to hundreds of millions of people around the world. Chicken Soup for the Soul's writers and readers belong to a one-of-a-kind global community, sharing advice, support, guidance, comfort, and knowledge.

Chicken Soup for the Soul stories have been translated into more than forty languages and can be found in more than one hundred countries. Every day, millions of people experience a Chicken Soup for the Soul story in a book, magazine, newspaper or online. As we share our life experiences through these stories, we offer hope, comfort and inspiration to one another. The stories travel from person to person, and from country to country, helping to improve lives everywhere.

Share with Us

We all have had Chicken Soup for the Soul moments in our lives. If you would like to share your story or poem with millions of people around the world, go to chickensoup.com and click on "Submit Your Story." You may be able to help another reader, and become a published author at the same time. Some of our past contributors have launched writing and speaking careers from the publication of their stories in our books!

Our submission volume has been increasing steadily—the quality and quantity of your submissions has been fabulous. We only accept story submissions via our website. They are no longer accepted via mail or fax.

To contact us regarding other matters, please

send us an e-mail through webmaster@chicken-soupforthesoul.com, or fax or write us at:

Chicken Soup for the Soul
P.O. Box 700
Cos Cob, CT 06807-0700
Fax: 203-861-7194

One more note from your friends at Chicken Soup for the Soul: Occasionally, we receive an unsolicited book manuscript from one of our readers, and we would like to respectfully inform you that we do not accept unsolicited manuscripts and we must discard the ones that appear.